An Wulin

**Translated by
Huaicun Zhang
Wang Dan**

Children Counting Stars

Young Paths

青岛出版集团 | 青岛出版社

This book is the result of a co-publication agreement between Qingdao Publishing House Co., Ltd. (CHINA) and Paths International Ltd (UK)

Title: Children Counting Stars
Author: An Wulin
Translated by Zhang Huaicun, Wang Dan
Hardback ISBN: 978-1-84464-710-1
Paperback ISBN: 978-1-84464-711-8
Ebook ISBN: 978-1-84464-712-5
Copyright © 2023 by Young Paths Childrens Books LTD.

青岛出版集团 | 青岛出版社
Young Paths Childrens Books LTD.
Paths International Ltd
www.pathsinternational.com
Published in United Kingdom

Children Counting Stars

An Wulin

Translated by
Huaicun Zhang
Wang Dan

Young Paths

青岛出版集团 | 青岛出版社

To seek for beauty, kindness and truth

—Preface of 'Children Counting for Stars'

In various literary styles, poetry has a natural connection with children. Children normally get closest to poetry as it inhabits their heart and is in the depth of their soul.

Children can learn poetry without a teacher because they have innocent feelings and rich imagination which are also the characteristics of poetry. Another characteristic is the musicality of poetry, the rhythm of which can directly reaching the soul and soothe it. Children can easily accept it through listening.

Children are born with innocence, imagination, and ability to listen to beautiful sounds. If children are given attention and enlightenment, they will know how to appreciate and listen to poetry.

We must work hard to take care of such poetic heart. When children are illiterate and unable to read the poems autonomously, they should be leaded into the "Poetry of Sound" that can be entered into their ears and rooted in their hearts. With the "Poetry of Sound" in mind, their hearing is comforted, which is also an artistic enjoyment. Therefore, we can say that the aesthetic taste of babies starts with sound; specifically, it starts with reading poems (children's rhymes). The children's rhymes can coordinate movements, add interest to the game, or even make children fall asleep peacefully as a lullaby. "Poetry of sound" is the first lesson in the initial aesthetic enjoyment of life. The rhythm of poetry is naturally integrated with poetry. Poems without rhythms are difficult to remember or spread.

When children can read independently, they have more choices. They can read myths, fairy tales, adventure stories, and fables. However, reading poems is also important at this time. Children's spiritual state and language expression ability can be enhanced by delight, charm, philosophical thinking, and subtle language expression in poems. Cultivating the pure interest of literature also depends on reading and appreciating poems.

We often say that poetry is literature in literature. We also say that literature is the foundation of various arts. The value of poetry is clearly demonstrated

by those comments. I once delivered," Reading poetry is not a general pastime, it can allow readers to get the joy and nourishment of reading from pure literary. The knowledge, such as emotions excited by music, feelings aroused by art painting, and enchantments from songs and dances, will make us understand the difference between reading poetry and reading other literary styles. "

We traditionally value poetic education which is always accompanied with emotions and deep-feelings.

Poetry offers us a keen eye to seek for beauty, that is, paying attention to life, nature and others. When finding beauty, our thoughts will be richer and our heart more abundant. Poetry also leads us continuously to explore the beautiful surroundings and to follow atmosphere in poetry with freshness and curiosity.

Poetry requests us to be kind. Reading poetry means communicating with the world, with the others, and with oneself, that is, perceiving harmony and sincerity, gasping gentleness and honesty, and understanding dignity and prestige. Excellent poems are a guide to kindness.

Poetry increases us the wisdom for truth. We will be touched and start to

meditate by reading poetry, and consequently have not only aesthetic taste but also power of critical thinking. Some poems are beautiful and creative, and some are sensible and vigorous. However, those particularly used as aphorisms, can even enlighten the mind and encourage people to pursue the truth.

In short, we will feel peaceful from reading poetry, understand life, enjoy life and encourage ourselves to build up a better life. We will also achieve triumph from reading poetry, gaining rich imagination that is even more powerful than the knowledge. People will be smarter, more sensible, and more ingenious in childhood if he is fond of poetry.

This set of poems in front of you is a well-crafted display of current children's poetry in China which contains all the characteristics of poetry I mentioned above, combining with beautiful words, fantastic pictures and lovely sounds.

I hope that all of you enjoy these poems.

Jin Bo

7th April 2017

Contents

Kid, please come with me

Kid, please come with me,
Bringing your spade,
And the basket.
Let's climb up the hill,
Where you can grow anything you like.
If you are not strong enough
To plant a tree,
Please sow the flower seeds instead.

Kid, please come with me,
Bringing your spade,
And the basket.
Let's climb up the hill,
Where you can grow anything you like.
If you are not strong enough
To plant a tree,
Please sow the grass seeds instead.

Kid, please come with me.

If nothing you enjoy planting,

Please look up at the clouds and birds in the sky,

The sun and streams in the valley,

And guess

What secrets they have already told to the tree hole.

Kid, please come with me.

Grass will turn green.

Flowers will bloom.

Bees and butterflies will visit again.

When the time comes,

Whatever you have already sowed,

The beauty thereafter will all belong to you.

Kid, please come with me,

Growing what you like.

The soil is rich,

And fertile.

It invites you

To plant anything,

Despite a wish to fly.

Stars on the ground

Stars are in the sky,

As lights

Shining in the dark,

As fireflies

Illuminating the roads for fairies

Who lose their way.

 However, there are some confused stars

Who carelessly

Lead fairies into bushes.

Although kids call them Winter Jasmine,

I still name them The Silly.

How lovely the stars are!

The charming stars

Occasionally direct fairies the way to land on the ground.

How careless the stars are!

Although kids call them dandelion,

I still name The Silly.

How cute the stars are!

The world is full of

Fairies and stars.

Who sometimes show up in your dream,

And sometimes play in the wind.

If you have a clear heart and bright eyes,

You will be one of the charming stars definitely.

Can I have a cuddle, Mum?

Mum, it is too cold.

I cannot feel my ears.

Mum says,

   - Come here. I will warm you up.

Mum, it is too cold.

I cannot feel my nose.

Mum says,

   - Come here. I will give you a kiss.

Mum, it is too cold.

I cannot feel my hands.

Mum says,

   - Come here. I will make you comfort.

Come here, my sweetheart. Let Mum embrace you.

   - No, Mum. I have grown up.

You can feel your ears, nose and hands again in Mum's arms.

   - Mum, yes, please. Can I have a cuddle?

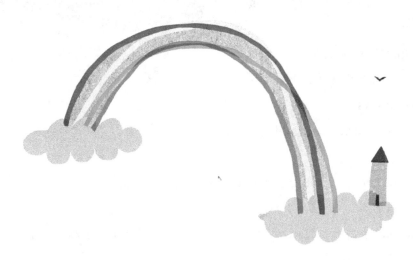

Climbing Plants

Climb up
Towards the sun,
And the sky.

It is shining
Continuously.
It is drizzling
Gently.

Climb up
Towards the sun,
And the sky.

Wiry tendrils as hands,
Twining stems as arms,
Are used to catch the sunlight
And embrace the rain.

Climb up
Towards the sun,
And the sky.

A Mushroom Pit

Under the tree,
There is a pit,
Where live five mushrooms.
They stand in a circle
To revel.

Is it a pit growing with mushrooms?
A mushroom pit.

It is perhaps the shower a few of days ago
Who brings the mushrooms here.
It is perhaps five butterflies
Or five busy bees
Who leave the mushrooms here.

A mushroom pit.

A pit growing with mushrooms.

Did five little stars visit last night

When I was deep in a sleep?

I was dreaming of the mushroom pit.

It is as round as my baby cradle

Where I can see Mum's joyful face

And recall my happy childhood.

Please clean your window

Lovely kid,
Please clean your window
To welcome the naughty sun.
It will turn to a book,
Sitting on your shelf.
It will become a pair of shoes,
Hiding under your bed.
It will change into a kiss,
Flying onto your face.
Hurry up, please clean your window.

A spacious room

A little mouse,
Living on the other side of the wall,
Makes a wish every night
To have a spacious room one day.

It tears up my socks,
Breaks off my shoes,
And destroys my chair and table.
It brings me too much trouble.

I go on a trip to get rid of it,
But I keep having nightmares.
I dream of all the relatives of the little mouse.
They make my room their wonderland.

When I return home,
I am surprised to find
A mummy cat rambling and playing
With her three kittens.

The little mouse is angrily shouting
On one side of the wall.
The mummy cat and her kids are happily dancing
On the other side.

Devil's Ginger

(It is sunroot, quite similar like gingers. It may be imported by the Germans when they encroached on Qingdao City in China. Chinese normally called invaders devils. Therefore, they named sunroots Devil's Ginger. —Remarked by the translator)

I cannot help laughing
When I initially hear your name.
I don't know who has so much humour
To name you in this way.
I thought you were sunflower when I was a kid,
And bitterly quarrelled with friends.
Your golden petals and round face
Are only a bit smaller than that of sunflowers.

I thought you were fruits of Ginger
As both of you look nearly the same.
The only difference is that Ginger is a seasoning,
While you are a real delicacy.

How annoying the name, Devil, is!
You feel unfair and refuse the name as soon as you were
born.
You dislike the name
Completely.
You are childish when you complain even if you are more
than three metres tall.

But you are imported, definitely.
You travel from North America, to Europe, and finally
throughout the world.

I really like you, deep in my heart.
I will water you, fertilise you, mow you, spray you and even
embrace you.

Frogs' Croaks

The night, with its sleepy eyes,
Cannot see my face clearly.
It urges me
To return to the bright room.

When I am passing by the lotus pool,
I suddenly hear frogs' croaks.
They are shouting
And croaking loudly.

Wind feels my heartbeats.

Roads recognise my footsteps.

Grass knows my breath.

Trees hear my shouts.

Where is the stone I used to skip across water?

Where is the paper boat I left in the pond?

Frogs are shouting

And croaking loudly.

I am fallen into memories of my childhood

By these pleasant frogs' croaks.

They save all my happiness

Under the leaves of lotuses.

A sleepless mouse

A little mouse
Is rolling on the bed
From one side to the other,
And rolling back again.

The sleepless mouse
Cannot close its eyes,
Rolling from one side to the other,
And rolling back again.

A kitten with a triangle face
Keeps meowing.
It wants to tickle the mouse
With its long whiskers
And sharp paws.
How bad the dream is!

Rolling from one side to the other,
And rolling back again.
Oops!
The mouse falls down onto the ground.
It lies underneath the bed
And goes on sleeping.
It laughs in the dream
As the kitten is only made of paper
Who is calling for help when falling into water.

Crawling

Slowly
Crawling
Is the morning glory
Up onto the shoulder of Evergreen.
It is so interesting.

slowly
Crawling
It seems that a lovely younger sister
Is draping her arms around her
brother's neck.
It is so interesting.

31

Listening

A squirrel is on a branch, listening
To chestnuts falling on the ground.
A seagull is on a reef, listening
To waves lashing against the rock.

Fungi are on trees, listening
To the forest roaring out.
Mushrooms are on grass, listening
To the dew dropping down.

Flowers are on the earth, listening
To the bright sun singing.
Boats are in the bay, listening
To the sparkling stars chatting.

A little child is cuddled in Mummy's arms, listening
To the love whispering
An old man is standing outside school, listening
To the childhood whistling.

Ears are like leaves, listening
To the breeze playing the violin.
Leaves are like ears, listening
To the birds twittering.

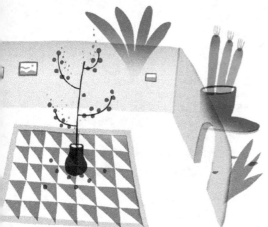

The mouse's house

The mouse's house
Is magnificent.
It has a lot of doors
Towards different places.

If you receive an invitation,
Please do accept it
As they never welcome
Any person trespassing.

I used to visit there
On a charming night.
I thought it must be dark and narrow,
But it was bright and spacious instead.

The mouse has a separate bedroom and kitchen,
And a large barn.
I had a look at all the rooms,
And thought I accidentally entered the wonderland.

The red carpet
Extended in all directions.
On the silver candlestick,
The candle was shining.

The wardrobe was full of tailcoats
Which, the mouse added, were worn when attending a ball.
Their family was a large one,
But everybody behaved as a gentleman.

Here were white tablecloth and silver dinnerware,

Together with meats, vegetables and delicious barbecue.

Here were ham and eggs,

Together with wines, liquor and appetising soups.

There was a secret room

That was for the mouse to pay tribute to the hero.

A huge portrait was hanging on the opposite wall,

In which stood a mouse who was even stronger than a rabbit.

The mouse said: this is my ancestor, who is an honoured hero

And used to be the King of the Kingdom of Cats.

The mouse was excited with glittering eyes

When recalling the family's glory in the past.

The mouse suddenly felt sad
And murmured that there has never been another mouse
Who could walk on the road in the Kingdom of Cats,
And who could lead to new success.

The mouse asked me to be an envoy of the Kingdom of Mice
As they would like to ally themselves with the cats.
When I sent the message to the cats,
They were as ferocious as tigers.

I have never been invited by the mice since then
Because they are scared of the smell of cats when I approach.
I long for the magnificent rooms of the mice
As well as their hearty food and warm welcome.

What is wrong with the trees?

What is wrong with the trees?
They are all pouting
Like little babies.

They push their lips forward.
They push their joints forward.
They push their chests forward.

They seem unhappy.
They seem angry.

Don't they wake up
From nightmare?
Don't they shake off
The cold in winter?

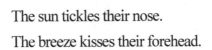

The sun tickles their nose.
The breeze kisses their forehead.

Everyone cannot help
But giggling.
All the leaves are wiggling.
All the blossoms are smiling.

Morning reading

In the morning,
The sun wakes up
And immediately
Opens a book.

The sun is looking at
Every leave passionately.
The sun is smiling at
Every petal happily.

High mountains,
Expansive oceans,
Hard rocks,
And silent deserts
Are all shining in the eyes,
And dancing on the lips, of the sun.

Birds are singing.

Dews are dropping.

The whole word starts morning reading.

Everybody has morning reading,

While the sun,

As the leading reader,

Speaks to all the children:

Join us please. Let's have morning reading together.

Speed up, Spring!

The downpour has
Very bad temper.
It drives away the haze
Directly.

The sun whistles loudly.
Ready, steady, go!
The sport games start.
How nice the weather is!

Come on, come on,
Speed up!
Come on, come on,
Speed up!

White roses open their little mouths.
Red roses open their little mouths.
Pink roses open their big mouths.
They all shout: Speed up, Spring!

The orchid is standing on its toes.
Willows are waving their hands.
Magnolias are playing trumpets.
Come on, Spring; Speed up, Spring!

Come on, come on.
The wind is applauding loudly.
He is the cheer leader,
Running together with Spring.

Begonia Road

Along the path
Stands begonia trees,
With red blossoms
And white petals.
They look like musical notes,
Gently telling their childhood secrets to the wind.

The boy
Picks up a flower quietly
And leaves it in the girl's pencil box.
He hopes she can be as lovely as a begonia flower.
The button is ripped out by tree sticks,
Leaving a small hole as a wound.
Hi Dad, please help me to find an excuse
To stop Mum from grumbling.

Along the path
Stands begonia trees,
With red blossoms
And white petals.
They look like musical notes,
Gently telling their childhood secrets to the wind.

The boy
Picks up a flower silently
And leaves it in the teacher's textbook.
He hopes she can be as beautiful as a begonia flower.
The back of his hand is scratched by tree sticks,
Leaving a wound as a track made by the ants.
Hi Mum, please help me to blow it
To stop Dad from frowning.

Along the path
Stands begonia trees,
With red blossoms
And white petals.
They look like musical notes,
Gently telling their childhood secrets to the wind.

Smiling

The green willow is swinging.
   - Isn't my waist flexible?
The dew dancing on the stamen
Is smiling.

The strong frog is croaking.
   - Isn't my voice loud?
The thunder walking on the other side of the hill
Is smiling.

The round soybean is rolling.
   - Isn't my fruit plump?
The peanut singing in the earth
Is smiling.

The cold wind is blowing.
   - Isn't my strength great?
The root practising push-ups under the tree
Is smiling.

The cool leopard is leaping.
   - Isn't my jump high?
The flea skipping on the back of the cow
Is smiling.

How wonderful the world is!
When the sun rises,
All the lives living on the earth
Are smiling.

An empty nest
-Writing to my child

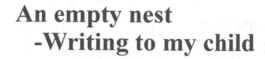

There is an empty nest
On the top of the tree.
The sun is curiously watching
And keeps touching the branches.

The bird used to sing in the nest.
The happy laughter has ever flown out.
But now, the moon is sighing quietly.
The stars are sparkling sadly.

The bird is flying away,
Just like the dandelion drifting in the sky.
The dews are left on the grass alone,
Tasting the flavour of the fall.

There is an empty nest
On the top of the tree.
The wind is roaming
With happy whistling.

I am looking up at the empty nest
And thinking of the bird faraway.
Does it have a warm straw hat
To wear in such a rainy season?

Sprouts in Spring

Spring's teeth are

Thin,

Sharp,

Fragile,

And tiny.

With them, the spring

Bites the dim sunlight,

Chews the soft moonlight,

And swallows the gentle starlight.

A few drops of dews,

And a couple of bird chirpings,

Can make the spring laugh continuously,

Just like a tiny stone in the water

Creating a number of ripples.

The clear air

Smells

Sweet.

There are always miracles happening in the world.

There are always miracles happening in the world.

The breeze cannot stop flowers from laughing.

The sunlight cannot stop drizzles from crying.

No matter it is happy or sorrow, fruits will ripen in the fall.

The fragrance in the air understands that all is real.

There are always miracles happening in the world.

The scarecrow cannot stop birds from singing across the plain.

The stars cannot stop voles from bustling in the wheat field.

No matter it is sweet or bitter, wheats will turn golden.

The moon in the sky understands that all is kind.

There are always miracles happening in the world.

Isolation cannot stop the stream from running.

Loneliness cannot stop the snowman from dreaming.

No matter it is smooth or harsh, the life will show their existence.

Old people and young children understand that all is beautiful.

There are always miracles happening in the world.

They are in the minds of people who always have dreams.

They are in the hearts of people who keep thinking positive.

They are in the life's journey of those who are brave and with love.

The Paulownia tree is flowering.

If winds run the fastest,
I would like to be one of them.

If the sun has the brightest eyes,
I would like to be a sunlight.

The Paulownia tree is flowering.
I must depart immediately.

Grandpa is hiding in the Paulownia tree with blossoms.
He enjoys playing hide-and-seek since I was a little kid.

One, two, three.
Every single paulownia flower looks like a tiny winecup.

Grandpa likes drinking the whole life.
He says he loves the feeling of wobbling and swaying.

Grandpa is on the verge of tears sometimes
When staring at the stars, or atching me going back home.

The paulownia tree is flowering.
All paulownia trees are flowering.

If the path is the most patient,
I would like to be part of it.

If cows are the most unbending,
I would like to be one of them.

Where is Grandpa hiding?
The paulownia flowers smell sweet.

He may hide in the hollow trunk of the paulownia tree.
If I smash with my fists,
Here will run out the liquor.

A small lawn

A small lawn
Belongs to me.
My entire world
Is that small lawn.

A cobblestone walkway
Meanders through the lawn
With roses and sunflowers standing on both sides,
Along which the ants are running happily.

The sun acts as an old dyer,
Turning the grass green,
The flowers red,
And my smiles golden.

In summer,
I lie down in the lawn,
Listening to cicadas chirping, and
Missing my home village.

My tiny world is shining
In a drop of a dew.
The small lawn is safe
To undercover all the secrets of my childhood.

The sun

The fleshy mushrooms
Are reciting your name.
The red cherries
Are missing you.

The plump lotus leaves
are reciting your name.
The crystal dews
Are missing you.

The round cobblestones
Are reading out your name.
The charming flowers
Are writing down your name.

The child with a chubby face
Is calling out your name.
The mother with a sweet smile
Is speaking to you in a tender voice.

All the lives
Are animated by you.
All the loves
Are awarded by you.

The earth is wafting
   -The sun's melodious voice.

A song of a potato

Hi, Mr. hairless,

How lovely

Your bald head is!

You used to be a perfect child,

Never crying, laughing, shouting or jumping

In Mummy's tummy.

What a well-behaved child you were!

But after you were born,

With your bald head,

You were wandering

From here

To there, and

Loitering from here

To there

You broke Mummy Hen's eggshells,

Destroyed Miss Mushroom's house, and

Scared away the kitten who was playing with the butterfly.

My goodness!

Do you think the potato is good?

With spring blossoms

With spring blossoms,

I will send postcards to my friends

To visit the village

Where I have been to school when I was young.

The sky is blue.

The air is fresh.

Stars and dewdrops look like clear eyes.

Wildflowers are as normal

As plain faces.

Perhaps I will deliver a lesson, and

Recall the pains and

The mischiefs

To make children laugh happily.

The sun is shining brightly.

It is the season of spring when all flowers bloom.

Expectation is warm and smells fragrant.

Perhaps I will feel ashamed of the test results when I was young,

And try to hide smartly.

But it doesn't matter.

I would like to make the children understand that

The winkles are as deep as the furrows

Where the wishes are planted,

And that smiles are the best remarks

For the life.

The spring has come and all the flowers are in bloom.

In such a wonderful season,

Every single child should sprout as the grass,

Be flowering, and

Sing with the bees.

The colour of the hometown

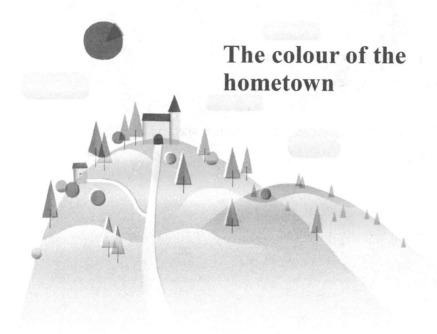

What is the colour of the hometown?

The hare replies,

It is green.

If you don't believe, please ask the grass in spring.

That is the colour of the hometown?

The bee replies,

It is red.

If you don't believe, please ask the roses in summer.

What is the colour of the hometown?

The vole replies,

It is golden.

If you don't believe, please ask the crops in autumn.

What is the colour of the hometown?

The sparrow replies,

It is white.

If you don't believe, please ask the chubby snowman in winter.

What is the colour of the hometown?

I reply,

It is colourful.

I you don't believe, please ask the girls' beautiful clothes.

Tiny Jujube flowers

Jujube flowers are as tiny
As millets,
swaying on the branches.

Their golden flowers are blooming
In clusters,
Laughing, playing and blushing.

Nobody understands
The secrets hiding
In their chuckling and whispering.

The sky is as blue as the lake.
The lake is as clear as the sky.
Their leaves are sparkling splendidly.

Days and nights in the countryside
Are quiet and calm,
Only the laughter of Jujube flowers wafting in the air.

Jujube flowers are as tiny
As millets,
Feeding up the happiness and astonishment in the childhood.
The Chinese dates look like fairies,
Swinging on the branches.
Here are the Jujube flowers, such tiny flowers.

Jujube flowers are as tiny
As millets,
Each of which has a wonderful fairy tale.

The sun is coming out.

The sun is coming out,
Startling the whole world.

The sparrow is panic,
Accidentally shaking off the snow on the branches.
The heavy snow fell yesterday
Filling in the ditches and covering the branches.

The sun is
Suddenly coming out,
Without any sign.

The curtain is opening its eyes,
And screaming.
Subsequent noises are
Floating out of the windows.

The slippery icicles on the ground
Make the busy ants keep falling down.
Only the wind knows
It is because the sun broke his mirror carelessly.

The sun is coming out,
Looking so grave.
It seems that he is carrying his bag
And running happily to the school.

Please come here, Mum!

Please come here, Mum!
A fly is
On my nose.
It says,
The girl
May be delicious.

My goodness! Mum,
Please come here!

Please come here, Mum.
A bee
Is on my nose.
It asks,
What kind of flower is it?
As it looks so strange.

Whoops! Mum,
Please come here!

Please come here, Mum.
A sunlight
Is shining on my nose.
It exclaims,
How cute the garlic is!
Please sprout quickly.

Hurrah! Mum,
Please come here!

The wind

The wind has bad temper
And is difficult to control.
It never stops
Or even slows down for a short time.

It kicks the tree,
Pokes the flower's nose,
And jumps in the river
To scare all the fish and shrimps.

The wind has bad temper
And is difficult to control.
It never stops
Or even slows down for a short time.

It kicks leaves into the pond,
Breaks the kite lines,
Blows the window paper,
And pretends to be a monster in the alley.

The wind
Is grumpy,
Blowing sand
Into the rabbit's eyes.

The wind
Is difficult to control,
Trying its best
To blow out the red lamps hanging on the Persimmon tree.

In winter,
It looks up and blows to the sky.
It keeps blowing
Bubbles.
How do the bubbles turn into snowflakes?
It doesn't know,
But only enjoys blowing
Up the snowflakes into the sky.

Miss Spring

Hey, Girl,

Please get up.

The ducks tickle you,

Making the whole lake ripple.

Hey, Girl,

Please get up.

The grass scratches your feet,

Making the moist earth wiggle.

Hey, Girl,

Please get up.

The sun keeps whispering in your ears,

Almost like a feather touching them.

Ah-ah-ah.
After a long yawning,
you rub the sleepy eyes.
Hey, Girl,
Your hair is so long and soft.
Please keep combing.

The beautiful flowers are all your mouths,
Making you keep murmuring.

The naughty child

The night
Is a naughty child,
Carrying lanterns made with fireflies
To walk from here
To there.

The lake
Looks like a large blanket.
By which the fish get their heads covered during sleep.
There are always active frogs
Who kick off the duckweed surrounding them.

The mouse is touching its whiskers.
The owl is glaring.
These two opponents
Never stop sleeping during the day,
But start to play hide-and seek when night falls.

How wonderful the world is!
It is noisy in the day,
But becomes very funny at night.
The naughty night accidently steps on some frog's foot,
Resulting in croaking throughout the pond.
He runs away immediately.

He cannot count
How many lanterns are lost.
But the number can be confirmed
By the stars in the sky, and
The fireflies in the lawn.

Flowers on the balcony

Whose balcony is it
That is full of flowers?
They enjoy talking to the people passing by,
Just like the lovely babies starting to speak.
Hello,
How are you?

The sun is smiling.
The moon is grinning.
The birds are chirping.
The bees are buzzing.

Hello,
How are you?

What are your names,
Flowers on the balcony?
Everyone has colourful face, and
A beautiful mouth.

Stop talking, and
Hold your tongue.

Is it the Cyclamen that is dancing?
Is it the Fuchsia that is swaying?
A little girl is watering with a spray.
Is the blush on her face made of roses?

Stop talking, and
Hold your tongue.

The little girl is smiling, and
Waving her hands.
But why her nails
Are so shiny?

What is that flower?
Why doesn't it hide its name?

The green train

Clanging, clanging,
The green train
Is coming with fierce appearance,
Like a green mantis.

Clanging, clanging,
The green train
Is coming with powerful appearance,
Like a green grasshopper.

Clanging, clanging,
The green train
Is coming with triumph,
Like a green frog.

Clanging, clanging,
The green train
Is coming with elation,
Like a scream in childhood.

A shoe is angry.

A shoe is angry,

Hiding in the corner under the table

In a far distance,

With its lips pouting,

Its body bending down, and

Its belly heaving.

The other shoe

Is calling it for a whole night.

Thought it shouts itself hoarse,

The shoe refuses to talk.

It is an angry shoe.

How horrible an angry shoe is!

It is made happy by the smiling eyes.
It is pulled gently by a hand.
It is kissed by a foot.
It then goes out pleasantly
To play with the other shoe.
How naughty you are!
How funny you are!

The wolf cub

The wolf cub is coming!

With the notice,
The whole village is in a mess.

The tree cannot find its staff,
Panting angrily.
The flower cannot find its comb,
Stomping anxiously.

The chicks are scared,
Shaking under the hen as trees swinging in the gale.
The piglets are startled,
Grunting besides the sow like the fierce bulls.

The wolf cub is coming!
The web woven by the spider is broken.
The colony made by the ants is destroyed.
The nest built by the hornets is fallen.
The cave excavated by the vole is submerged.

The grass and trees in the village
Are withered as suffering malaria.
The birds and animals in the village
Are crazy as suffering mania.

The wolf cub is coming!

It is encircled by the children,
Just like stars surrounding the moon.
Naughty kids like to chase anything naughty,
Just like a flock following the bellwether.

The adults are raising their hands,
But hating to punch the wolf cub.
When people in the village calling his name—the wolf cub,
They always enjoy looking up into the sky.

Cole flowers

After stars have played hide-and-seek in the cole fields,
Cole flowers resemble stars.
After the sun has had a rest among cole flowers,
The sunlight smells fragrant.

Hi, the beautiful cole flowers.

After butterflies have held a ball here,
Cole flowers dance gracefully.
After bees have sung a song here,
Cole flowers develop a clear voice.

Hi, the beautiful cole flowers.

Who dyes the golden colour for you?
Isn't it done by the sun,
The stars,
Or the dream of childhood?

Hi, the beautiful cole flowers.

September

The duck is waddling
Without tightening its shoelaces.

The willow tree is walking gracefully,
Without combing its hair.

Flowers are coming joyfully,
Without stopping their conversation.

The frog is hopping happily
After doing its homework for the whole summer.

The wind is singing and approaching,
After running around for the whole summer.

The green grass
Is rambling rapidly.

Nobody knows how many poems done by the stars
Have been picked up by the fish in the pond
In such a long summer holiday.

Nobody knows how many calculations
The hardworking ant has practised
On the ground.

Both triumph and remorse
Have hidden secretly as the dewdrops on the leaves.

September is coming.
September is showing up in the melody.

Eyes in a tree

There is a pair of eyes
In a tree,
Looking at another tree
Where there is an ant
And a snail,
Crawling slowly
Towards a leaf,
The sunshine,
And the chirping cicadas.

91

There are pairs of eyes

In trees,

Looking into the eyes of each other to see

Their smiles,

Promises,

And secrets.

They also see the fascinating moon,

And hear the interesting conversations between stars.

Beauty in the world

Needs finding out by the eyes.

A tree has a pair of eyes.

Trees have pairs of eyes.

Little ears

There are many little ears
In the world
Listening.

A mushroom is an ear of the earth,
Listening
To the growth of a tree.

A petal is an ear of Spring,
Listening
To the flying of bees and butterflies.

The moon is an ear of the sky,
Listening
To the food transferring by hamsters.

A child is an ear of Mum,
Listening
To the love in the world

The more little ears are in the world,
The more wonderful secrets,
And charming sounds there will be.

Childhood is a habitat for poetry fairies.

Poetry belongs to childhood, juveniles, and young adults, whom the most energetic life and the most passionate life belong to. Poetry is dedicated to them.

Poetry is a fancy, fancying anything beautiful. Human expectation, expectancy, reveries, and reverence essentially belong to the category of poetry.

Because of fancies, flying in the sky finally comes true. Therefore, poetry is like a dandelion, growing on the earth, but her ultimate goal is to fly in the sky and towards far distance.

Only poetry has such elements as brevity and elegance. It both gazes affectionately and overlook arrogantly at the earth. There is no more complex style than it.

Children's poetry has its own special composition. Children's innocence, taste and fun are essential. It is even more important that it is clear, soft, bright, optimistic and cheerful. As long as there is a trace of melancholy, it

will grow up to become a poem for teenagers to express their feelings. Children's poetry is a natural thing, just as the land inseparable from plants. What can be separated is not a children's poem. Excessive pursuit of poetry skills is as uncomfortable as the behaviours of the precocious children.

I believe that truth, kindness and beauty are the soul of poetry, especially for children's ones. If we cannot provide such soul, no matter how excellent the poem is, we should never show to the children. They can wait to appreciate gradually after they grow up. As soon as a child comes into the world, he is stuffed with a lot of things, even if the whole world. They have no choice. We should provide them what suits them and what they are fond of. This is care, companionship, responsibility, and the mission of each poet in children's poetry.

Turgenev was a great novelist. He said in his early years: "Poetry is the language of God. I also like poetry. But poetry is not just in verses, poetry is everywhere and encircles us ... Please look at these trees and the sky—there is beauty and life everywhere. Where there is such beauty and life, there is poetry! "He expressed his understanding of poetry through the mouth of Rudin. Years later, he finished the popular work "Front Cover", which was

a practice and a return.

No matter it is the sun, the sky, the white clouds, the mountains, the sea, the lawn, the wildflowers, the children's laughter and their running figures, or their dreams, they are all the habitats for poetry fairies. The world is full of melody of poetry and pictures of poetry. The mission of us, the poets in children 's poetry, is to discover and express them. All beautiful things are the elements of poetry.

The appreciation of beauty is a training of children's sense functions. The smaller thing the children are gazing at and paying attention to, the better sense function they have. Therefore, I will try my best to improve the children's ability to appreciate beauty. I hope that "Children Counting Stars" will provide them with some thinking and surprise.

Jin Bo
7th April 2017